JERRY MITCHELL

TRADITION *to* TRUTH

One Man's Search For Honest Answers

Ordering Information:

Books to Life Marketing Ltd
128 City Road, London, EC1V 2NX, UK

Printed in the United States of America

*Howbeit in vain do they worship me,
teaching for doctrines the commandments
of men. For laying aside the commandment
of God, ye hold the tradition of men, as the
washing of pots and cups: and many other
such like things ye do*
Mark 7; 7–8

INTRODUCTION

When my dear lovely wife made the offhand suggestion that I write a book I thought she had lost her mind. She told me that people need to see things in writing not just hear them and she is right, being cynical I check everything I hear and a lot of what I read. After trying to put the thought out of my mind ideas began to surface in my head then on pages in my computer.

I thought some background was necessary and the first few pages are just that, allowing the reader to identify with the writer. I know I can't be the only person who wants to know the truth that is contained in the pages of the Bible and what I discovered is only a beginning to learning more.

Many commentaries have been written about what passages mean to those who write them, I didn't care what they meant to anyone with the exception of the creator. Sifting through books, internet sites and compiling a list of reference material left me confused and disillusioned. Years of sitting through the same Lectionary sermons delivered by the most well intentioned pastors who were parroting their teachers couldn't satisfy the desire I had to stop drinking the milk and Kool-Aid, and wean myself into the meat of scripture.

I attempted to make this easy to read and understand for everyone who might be bored enough to actually read this, so if you are twelve or one hundred twelve you can get through it. I purposely did not to include a lot of technical information, there are many sources to choose from which are written by people who have been studying scripture far longer than I have.

There is on purpose some grammatical and spelling free license used for my personal preference which in my humble opinion does not detract from the ideas I am trying to relay.

I encourage you to use your Bible as a companion to this book, look up the scripture for yourself and study it. Don't be afraid to ask, "What does this mean?" Then search for the answer, just be careful, the answer you get might not be what you expect.

1

*Train up a child in the way he should go
And when he is old he will not depart from it*
Proverbs 22; 6 (King James)

BEING RAISED AS an east coast farm boy, brought up in a traditional Methodist family, would lead most to believe that I should have been content to go with the conventional flow. That would have been too easy, too comfortable and too convenient. I believed what was in my school books and much as I hated school, it was a necessary evil to sit through class all day looking forward to the last bell when I could get outside and be free. Living on a small farm had its advantages; there were trees to climb, fields to explore chickens to be harassed and chores to be done. There were a lot of life lessons to be learned on that farm too, baby chicks come from eggs, grow into big chickens and eventually end up as Sunday dinner. Plants need to be watered and weeded and the fruits need to be harvested. I liked dealing with the animals more than the vegetables and grain we raised, you don't have to stand in the hot sun pulling weeds around chickens, just feed and water them and pick up the eggs. Keep their house clean and they do the rest. Life is easy when you're ten.

Church and Sunday school were important, Saturday afternoon was the trip to the barber, then after supper shoes had to be shined and baths were next on the agenda. Sunday morning breakfast was served with the radio on listening to the Bible stories from Grand Rapids, then off to church all dressed up and a stern warning not to scuff those shoes. Sunday school was first, I was expected to be well behaved there, my mother was the teacher. She and another lady would have us sing or tell us stories or color some picture with people in robes or wearing wings, I still have a hard time overcoming those images when studying Biblical culture and history. Sitting in the service I learned quickly to sit next to Dad, he would let me get away with a lot more squirming and sometimes I thought he was wondering the same thing I was, just how much longer can this guy talk!

Christmas was special at church, fancy decorations and candles in the windows and of course the properly displayed Nativity with a borrowed doll wrapped in swaddling clothes asleep in the hay. Everyone seemed a lot nicer at Christmas; people didn't mind children running around getting in the way, being excited and telling anybody who would listen what we wanted that year. For some reason celebrating the birth of Jesus was not as important as a whole ten days away from school and getting to play with all the new toys.

The time just before Easter was different too, the music was like a funeral and there was a lot of black. That is until Easter morning when the Easter bunny came to get us all "sugared" up and wild as mountain goats. The songs were happy about "Up from the Grave" and "Because He

Lives." There was a white cloth on the cross and the people must have forgotten about Christmas because they were back to giving the usual commands of "don't run" and whispering "children should be seen and not heard."

That's how I grew up, just like most other American kids. I was lucky, I had three older brothers to break in my parents for me and I had to really try to come up with something new they had not already been through. That was a challenge I was suited for, I was the daredevil. I found out early that gravity works the same way all of the time and nothing works like it does in the movies. I was also stubborn, when something didn't work as planned just tweak the design and try again, to this day I know that bed sheet parachute would have worked if that barn roof had been taller.

Lucky, no! I was blessed beyond compare! I was sure I had an entire army of guardian angels assigned to me personally and thankfully they are still on duty. My escapades would be good training for army ranger school but they have too many safety requirements to benefit from the dumb stuff I did growing up (by the way I'm still growing up.)

Yea, I had a really blessed childhood and that continued through my teens. The Creator of the universe for some reason decided to smile on me, even when I was caught up with other things like girls, or the guitar, or horses, or girls, SCUBA diving, girls, work, girls, you get the picture.

No matter where I was or what I was involved with whatever I was looking for kept me returning to the Bible, it was the one constant in a quickly changing world. I could read it but didn't understand it, I thought there must be some mysterious code in there that only preachers understand but wouldn't share. As much as I hated school I had a passion for learning, hands on, if I could take it apart I could put it back together but I couldn't get this Bible thing apart. There was too much there that didn't make sense and if I asked ten people what something meant I got ten different answers. If this God thing is real there can only be one correct answer, if God did create the Heavens and the Earth and he did do everything the Bible tells us he did, why hide it in a code? What was I missing? I didn't know how to explain what I wanted to know, I just wanted to know the truth. Something was definitely missing.

For as in the days that were before the flood they were eating and drinking, marrying and giving in marriage, until the day that Noah entered into the ark
Mathew 24; 38 (king James)

MARRIAGE TAKES UP a lot of time when you're young and trying to figure out why any normal person would put themselves through the agony of adjusting to living with some stranger. My first marriage wasn't much fun at all, there were some good times spent with friends but I wouldn't change my attitude and she didn't either. I found out there are really four sides to every story like this;

1. What he said or did
2. What she said or did
3. What everyone else thinks was said or done
4. The truth.

People today are not taught how to be married. I learned the hard way what not to do and what shouldn't happen. People are not born with an instinct for how to get along with each other, we simply do the best we can with the little information we have. Failing at marriage is easy, making a long lasting commitment is difficult. Marriage is not a 50/50 partnership, both people must be willing to give 100% to the relationship or it will fail. There may be positive outcomes from a failed marriage but divorce isn't something to look forward to. When my first marriage was ending I went back to church and did my best to remain as faithful as Job did during his time of trouble.

Divorce is a circus with the judges as ringmasters and lawyers the performing monkeys and the only ones who will feel the effects are treated as the clowns. That is what happens when a religious institution ends in a civil court; the only people who gain anything are the lawyers and the courts. Although I did regain my freedom from the oppressive hand of satan, like Job I did my best to stay faithful to the creator and was rewarded for that.

Starting over wasn't all bad, I had the freedom to choose where I went and with whom I went. I was able to find a better job and gained too much weight eating my own cooking. After a few months I decided to get back into my skinny clothes and began a ritual of running and other exercises. Work, working out, goofing off from time to time and beginning to date again, there was also time for hunting, fishing and friends. Where I lived I received only three TV stations, since I was hardly home I didn't waste money for cable.

I kept busy and even went back to church occasionally, usually to play my guitar and sing the special music portion of the service but the message was always the same no matter which church I went to," live to love and love to give." From what I could understand, every church thought they were the only ones who had the path to Heaven. Just give them enough money to convince the rest of the world and all would be saved just by hearing the word of their preacher. I was really getting a bad taste in my mouth for organized religion, more of the same dribble being spewed for the comfort of the most generous fillers of the offering plate. Something was still missing and I had no clue why I wanted to find out what it was but didn't know where to begin.

3

> *Blessed is the man that endureth temptation:*
> *for when he is tried, he shall receive the crown*
> *of life, which the Lord hath promised to them*
> *that love him*
>
> James 1; 12 (King James)

WHEN I FIRST met this innocent looking lady who would eventually become my second wife, marriage was the last thing I wanted to be involved with again. She was working in the convenience store where I would stop to get my cupcakes and milk on the way to work in the morning. We would exchange pleasantries since I was a regular. One day I had been on an errand and she wondered why I was late. I jokingly said I needed to be measured for a funeral suit for a friend of mine. With the deepest sympathy in her voice she said "I'm sorry, how old was he?" I explained she didn't understand, a good friend of mine was getting married and I was in the wedding and went to be measured for a tux. After that our conversations lasted a little longer until the day I asked if she would like to go to dinner. "I'm not dating men," was the answer, "Oh?

OK" I really wasn't expecting that answer, no would have been good enough, she realized I didn't understand and said she wanted some space after a divorce and another bad relationship. No problem, I continued to come in and get my milk and cupcakes, exchange pleasant conversation but didn't even hint at a date. I guess she knew I wasn't going to ask again because a few weeks later I had a phone call at work, she had won tickets to a dance and asked if I wanted to go. After giving several milliseconds of thought to the idea I agreed to go. That was twenty five years ago (as of the time I write this) and have not had another first date since.

I found out she was a preacher's kid, her father a Baptist pastor who also had served in the mission field while she was a child and took the family with him to St. Lucia. My new sweetheart learned how to eat some strange things where she grew up. I kept hearing about fish eye gravy and green bananas. She had a boy and a girl from her first marriage and we seemed to get along just fine. I visited her church but was fast to realize they were no different than any of the others. As we were planning our wedding the Methodist church I liked the most had a new pastor, about six months older than I am and fresh out of the cemetery, I mean Seminary. I like Randy he was naïve and innocent but smart. He had a way of explaining things that made more sense than most others and so the new family and I began to attend regularly and I wound up teaching Sunday school. Yes we were the typical American family, working five days and spending Sunday morning in church and Sunday afternoon with either her parents or mine. What more could I ask for?

Adventure! Since I had visited the western states in my teens, I wanted to explore. I was a fair hand with horses and cattle and knew my way in the outdoors. A family vacation through the Midwest was Ok but didn't satisfy the desire to be truly free, be my own man, to be out where the coyotes howl. After a trip for me to the big sky country of Montana, I came home packed up the family and moved to Colorado. A state with just a little more population and I thought it would be more fun for the children. I went to work as a hunting guide, there is a certain amount of satisfaction being able to take people into the wild and bring them back safely. Unfortunately, this first excursion didn't work out and we wound up back on the east coast for a while until we just couldn't stand it anymore.

Back to Colorado we went, working on a guest ranch and having a great time with the guests, but God had other plans. We made contact with a cattle ranch in North Park and went to see the operation. Soon we were up there working, I had finally found a place I fit in, hardworking, honest people and great country to explore. I don't know what I ever did to deserve that reward but it was worth every bump in the road to live that dream.

Yes, I was still blessed, and still there was something missing. We went to town to church when we had the time. We visited a couple of churches, one I really wish we hadn't; the pastor said I had no respect for the house of the Lord because I wasn't wearing a tie around my neck. Those bad feelings about religion were coming back. I had been so busy working on the ranch that church didn't cross my mind much, I had every chance to talk to God right out there in the country he made, sitting on a horse, cattle around me and God above smiling down. I had everything I wanted, I thought.

4

Honor thy father and thy mother:
that thy days may be long upon the land
which the Lord thy God giveth thee
Exodus 20; 12 (King James)

WITH PARENTS AGING I was beginning to feel like Jonah, being needed to go back home but doing everything I could to continue to stay in Colorado. My wife and I both love the mountains, no humidity and the way of life we had on the ranch. She noticed first that we should move back to honor our mothers and fathers. She was the one who spoke to them more often than I did and I really didn't want to admit there was anything wrong with them. I lived with that feeling of denial for about seven or eight months until a phone call got my attention. We made the arrangements then picked up, packed up and moved back to the beach.

What we found when we got back was not what we were hoping to find. My parents were enjoying good health when we left but time and age had caught up to them especially Dad. He had what we thought was the onset of Alzheimer's, or the beginning stages of dementia at least. Mom was doing her best to care for him and cover the worst of the symptoms. My mother, always the controlling influence, kept her usual "I know what's best for everybody" mentality and it was difficult for her to allow any of us to help care for them. Dad had always called her a hard headed Dutchman, in reference to her Lancaster Pennsylvania roots. The only way to help was to make her think it was her idea and that wasn't an easy task.

My wife's parents were somewhat younger than mine and were still in reasonably good health considering her father having diabetes and her mother having a history of health issues. This gave us time to concentrate on my parents while finding jobs to pay our bills and get used to living in a beach resort again. Traffic was the worst thing to use to, I hate it! I have driven all over the country and still believe the worst traffic problems are in the beach resorts where I grew up. Then there were old friends to catch up with and of course going back to church.

That small church we left had grown, really grown. They had talked about a larger building for years but now they were ready to get serious about actually breaking ground. We had been active there before and were expected to continue when we returned. I went back to playing in the praise band and agreed to serve on a committee. The building process began and we were somewhat involved with that as well. About a year later, the new building was consecrated and things were going as well as possible getting adjusted to the new building.

So far everything in my life seemed to fit into the traditional lifestyle that everybody would have expected, (with the exception of an adventurous spirit.) Growing up, celebrating birthdays, Christmas, Easter and being a responsible family man and a fine upstanding member of the community. I fit the all-around American stereotype if there is one, but still there was something missing.

Most people feel it and look for it in the strangest places like an adulteress relationship or in a bottle or some type of drug; I have come to believe it is that spirit in most of us that is trying desperately to connect with the Holy Spirit of the Creator. In each person there is something so small that we don't notice it. A whisper or a feeling that begins as an annoyance, like a loose button on a shirt but then it becomes a small stone in your shoe. That inconvenient annoyance begins to get larger, some people might think it is a health issue or other problem with their life; they might blame a spouse or a child and look for relief with a prescription. Some may self-diagnose it as needing to change their occupation; friends may tell them they just need a vacation or give other unwanted and bad advice. Fortunately, I had a good idea what the source of this feeling was; I always had questions that I thought there were no answers for. I talked to pastors, both present and past. I searched out people I thought would be able to give me that secret formula to decode the mysteries of the Bible but that didn't help much at all. I didn't realize it then but God had already put the people in my life a long time ago that had been gently nudging me to go find the answers I craved.

Gather the people together, men and women, and children, and thy stranger that is within thy gates, that they may hear, and that they may learn, and fear the Lord your God, and observe to do all the words f this law
Deuteronomy 31; 12 (King James)

SOMETIMES, EVEN THE most simple idea can begin a chain of events that can't be stopped. One thing leads to another and before you know it you're out of the frying pan and diving headfirst into the fire. I had met someone who was teaching at our vacation Bible school who was studying to be a Messianic Rabi, I had heard of the Messianic congregations but didn't think much about it (I was taught to think they were just Jews who believed in the Jesus) this wonderful lady made the comment that one of the reasons the Bible was hard to read was because of some of the loose translations from the original text. My bright idea was that if I could learn Hebrew and get the language barrier out of the way I might be able to better understand what the Bible was all about.

I began an off the wall self-study in the Hebrew language, take my advice here; don't try it this way. I was never very good at foreign language, just ask my high school Spanish teacher. Finally I tried one of the "learn a foreign language" courses on CD, what a difference that made. Just inset a CD and in no time I actually began to understand and speak Hebrew. Not a lot at first, but with time and concentration I was able to pick up the fact that there are words in Hebrew that don't have a word for word English translation. Some Hebrew words may take a paragraph to explain in English. Hebrew like many languages is a language of action and ideas, things need to be read over more than once to get the proper context.

The next problem I encountered was the cultural difference; I was used to my American culture and thought the world revolved around it. I was wrong, not only is the Hebrew way of thinking different but is different today than it was two thousand years ago and even that is different than it was three thousand years ago. That meant a new study in history to go along with the language study.

In my mind if you want to lean about Hebrew history read a Hebrew historian and that meant reading Josephus. His history is the book most historians reference when they study, so it should be good enough for me. If I had one subject in school I liked more than any other it was history so reading Josephus was enjoyable for me. I am not the typical person when it comes to reading, I like reference books and technical reading anyway. Eusebius, was next on the list, although not as enjoyable to read there is a lot of information in that book and I had never heard any of it referenced in any sermon. Philo, was interesting and difficult even for me to read to the end but it did give some insight to the way the people of that time period were thinking.

Language, history and culture I was becoming a pastor's worst nightmare, just enough knowledge to have even more questions while being able to point out flaws in their sermons. I had a new understanding for the word of God and was able to decipher some of the "code" which wasn't code at all, just poor translation in some places combined with human error in other places.

I discovered something I had never heard of before, an Interlinear Bible. This new discovery has the Hebrew and Greek with phonetically transliterated English under it and the typical verse beside it. What a way to translate! I also used the 1611 King James, New International Version and the Complete Jewish Bible for reference. The next big question was; why had nobody told me about these things before?

I had the chance to speak with an orthodox Rabi on a Friday afternoon. He and his family were preparing for their Sabbath so I didn't have a lot of time and had to choose my questions for him carefully. A meeting I'm sure was arranged through divine intervention. Armed with a new way of looking at the Hebrew language from a Jewish point of view I was developing a picture in my mind that reading the Torah in Hebrew wasn't like reading a book, it was holding a conversation with the creator. In Hebrew, there are the nuances, the body language so to speak, of the writer. Meaning is not only communicated through the words but the letters that are there and sometimes the letters that are not used in a word, phrase or passage. There are four concepts to reading the Bible they are the literal, the metaphorical, the implied and the hidden. When we stop just reading and have that two way conversation we begin to understand the spirit of what God is telling us, this is even possible when we read it in English most of the time.

An example that works well in English from Genesis 9; 20–21, Noah leaves the ark with his family. The next thing we learn is Noah became a farmer, then he gets drunk; this is the literal, or what we read in those 2 verses. How many years were necessary for grape vines to grow into a vineyard are not described in the literal; meaning we don't exactly know but we do know these are real people, living real lives and the intricate details are left for us to uncover. Metaphorically, I believe we can suggest that Noah was providing for his family and teaching his sons and their wives to do the same. What is being implied is that life goes on; people eat sleep and go through their daily routine of living. The hidden meaning in these verses may go far beyond even what anyone has considered but there is a wink and a nod in them from the creator letting us know there is much more to these verses. Something lies in them that we need to examine this life lesson more closely.

What kind of relationship did Noah have with the Creator? Did Noah question God's decision to flood the earth and was his complete obedience blinding him from some of his personal issues he needed to pray about? Did Noah make sure all of his sons understand who God is and they need to trust God to survive in this renewed world they now live in? These questions can only be answered in the surrounding Scriptures of the verses. Take the time to examine the lesson of Noah, from his birth to his death. Don't just read it, slow down and question exactly what happens and why. I think you might find some very interesting people in Noah's life, who he was able to talk to and who influenced him to be the one that God chose to build the ark.

For the first time in my life at least, that something missing feeling was beginning to be satisfied while at the same time I had a new feeling of being misinformed about a whole lot of "churchy" things. Studying the Bible the way I had stumbled onto really was bringing me closer to God but it was pushing me further from my "Religion." The answers I found were certainly not the answers I wanted or expected. I was looking for proof that everything I had been taught in Sunday school was just fine and dandy. I wanted to be comfortable with all the things I thought were true and continue to live that traditional life I had. That couldn't happen with the answers I had now. There were too many things that didn't conform to what I had been taught to believe.

6

Remember the Sabbath and keep it Holy
Exodus 20; 8 (King James)

THE FIFTH COMMANDMENT; remember the Sabbath, a lesson that lasted 40 years. Here is where my traditions began to come apart. I was brought up to believe that Sunday had always been the Sabbath but I was wrong. I believed it because that is what I was taught. My Grandfather displayed a copy of a letter from the church he went to that was supposed to have been written by Jesus. One sentence in that letter read *"have your work done by 6:00 on Saturday so you will be ready for the Sabbath."* I really didn't think about that until I changed from reading the Bible to Studying the Bible. What good first century Jewish man would write that? Not any of them, especially not the Torah keeping Messiah! Churches around the world meet on Sunday, why? Because according to tradition Jesus rose on Sunday. Only according to tradition, Scripture tells a different story but you need to understand the culture of the people in the first century to find out how.

Telling time wasn't always as easy as looking at your watch or glancing at a calendar. Unlike today, time was told by Bells or when the watchmen would change shifts (hence the term watch for a timepiece.) days began at sundown, not the stroke of midnight, how could you tell of it was 12:00Am with no timepiece and the sun on the other side of the earth? Days were numbered but accounts were kept by who was in charge and the Hebrew accounts by who was in the temple. This Sunday Sabbath comes from a combination of misinterpretation of language and culture mixed with a good measure of death threats from Emperor Constantine during his reign. If you read the scripture carefully, there is a mathematical equation between the New Testament account of the crucifixion and the Passover feast which places the resurrection on the real Sabbath (Saturday.)

Matthew 28; 1 reads that after the Sabbath (Saturday at sunset) at dawn on the first day of the week (Sunday) Mary went to the tomb. Jesus didn't rise at sunrise on Easter morning; he was up and had been in seclusion then working, gathering the saints for the first fruit offering. Mary shows up at the tomb long after the Roman soldiers left their post, didn't you ever wonder what happened to them? Not convinced yet? I will encourage you to read it for yourself, look at all of the surrounding and related scripture and keep it in the proper context and see for yourself. Did you ever wonder why Jesus used a colt, an untrained little jack donkey for his triumphant entry into Jerusalem? That little critter had not done any work in its life and was able to spend his first day on the job on the Sabbath! Remember, "six days you shall work," then you get to rest on the Sabbath. No, that doesn't mean if you have a vacation and return home on Friday that it is OK to work on the Sabbath. And it surely doesn't indicate that you can have any day of the week off just to suit your schedule.

We are a community and God has given us His instructions for a reason. The Sabbath rest is one of the most misunderstood provisions in the Bible. There are churches whose doctrine is to preach that the church has removed the Sabbath from the authority of Heaven. According to the Catechism of Catholic doctrine, the church changed the Sabbath during the Council of Laodicea in 336 AD. Basically the church has attempted to steal the authority to change God's word from the Creator Himself. Jesus warned his followers in his last public appearance at the temple not to listen to or follow these man made rules (the *Heavy burdens and grievous to be borne* in Matthew 23) when he said "Do what Moses said to do."

Who will you choose to follow? Men are only human; they lie, cheat and steal to gain the appearance of being in charge of your life. Most American politicians enjoy the spotlight and glamour of their position. Our founding Fathers meant for public service to be like a curse or disease, something to be avoided if possible and certainly not sought after. Unfortunately, today people have a desire to be elected to public office; they want the popularity, power and easy money. The Messiah offers so much more than any of these things. Jesus offers us a chance to be all we can be, to live to our full potential on earth and then be rewarded later in Heaven.

My Sunday day of rest tradition was shattered but at least I understood why. Finally an answer to a question that had not only solid Biblical foundation but historical facts to prove why we disregard God's instructions and I have only offered just a few of those. What other traditions are we keeping that the Bible tells us we shouldn't? Did I dare to find the next answer? YES

*O Lord, my strength, and my fortress,
and my refuge in the day of affliction,
the Gentiles shall come unto thee from the
ends of the earth, and shall say, Surely our
fathers have inherited lies, vanity, and things
wherein there is no profit*
Jeremiah 16; 19 (King James)

JEREMIAH 16; 19, reads in part; "surely our fathers have inherited lies." If our fathers were given lies concerning the scriptures how could they pass the truth on to our generation? Were they more at fault for believing the lies or for failing to scrutinize what they were told? We can ask the same of ourselves. The harsh reality is we must carefully examine what we are taught and compare that to what is written in the Bible in order to know the character of the teacher. It is responsibility to find the false prophets in our assemblies, to correct them if they will listen to the Holy Spirit and cast them out if they will not. Shaul (Paul) tells us in 1 Corinthians 5; 21 Prove everything and keep what is good. No person I know wants to accuse any other of wrongdoing especially when it comes to scripture. They might gossip about what a teacher or preacher said or worse accuses a brother or sister of some crime like not sweeping the floor after a church social but to question false teaching; Heaven Forbid!

I have learned to scrutinize everything, listen carefully and study what was said. I have since learned to recognize blatant misinformation and often question it (at the appropriate time.) We need to make a commitment to follow scripture not tradition and ritual. I could climb to the top of a building and cry out all day that two plus two equals five but it would be a lie and a lie cannot magically become truth no matter how many people begin to believe the lie. By climbing that building and making that statement every day I would have created a tradition through ritual. That doesn't make it right, true or the sane thing to do. So how does a lie become a tradition in a body of those who think they are dedicated to following the savior? No one bothered to question the lie or they were forced to accept it.

In Ezekiel 8; 14 we read about women weeping for Tammuz, when this was written everyone knew who Tammuz was. Many eastern cultures today know who he was but the western Christian doesn't. Why? We were never taught about it Sunday school. Tammuz was a sun god (the offspring of Nimrod's widow, Semiramis) who was killed by a wild boar when he was forty years old. (Some god, gored to death by a pig) His followers began the tradition of giving up a pleasure in this life so he would have pleasures in heaven; the time of mourning began forty days (one day for each year or his life) before the spring equinox, just in time for Easter. Does this tradition sound familiar? Have you been weeping for Tammuz and calling it lent? Have you accepted the lie that you are getting ready for Passion Week? STOP! Don't keep doing it! It's bad for your health.

Deuteronomy 12; 4 tells us not to use pagan rituals to worship the creator *"**Do not worship the LORD your God in their {pagan} way**"* (NIV with addition). He calls it an abomination, in case you didn't know that's a really, really bad thing. We were instructed not to learn the ways of the pagans, not to know their gods or their rituals. We were to tear down their alters, destroy their idols and forget all about them, so what happened? Human history, life gets in the way and we think we are smarter than God. Instead of doing what God said we add to it. Look at Eve in the garden for an example; God said," Don't eat the fruit from that tree." That's what he told them, just don't eat it, they could have picked it up and thrown it for the other animals to fetch, the only thing they couldn't do was eat it. So when Eve was talking to the snake what did she do? She added to what God said, "We shouldn't even touch it," That's when things went downhill quick, fast and in a hurry for the rest of us and why we are instructed in Deuteronomy 4; 2 ***Do not add to what I command you and do not subtract from it, but keep the commands of the Lord your God that I give you*** (NIV) Only if Eve would have said something like "God told us not to eat it so I won't." she could have left it right there and today we would either be living in the garden or blaming somebody else for the fall of man.

What is the fascination we have with adding to God's word? Have we become as arrogant as to think we can run the universe when we can't keep our own lives in order? Yes, we have and the results are showing up in churches, schools and the rest of society today. Pagan rituals have become accepted as the only way to worship in our churches. We celebrate pagan holidays and think we are celebrating the

Creator, the Methodist church which I was a part of for a long time has turned its back to scripture. The Baptist church has marched right along beside as I am sure all of the other denominations have. All of this has happened because we failed to remain vigilant, scrutinize the teachers and accepted the lies which we inherited.

Howbeit in vain do they worship me, teaching for doctrines the commandments of men. For laying aside the commandment of God, ye hold the tradition of men, as the washing of pots and cups: and many other such like things ye do. Mark 7; 7–8 (King James)

When asked about the ritual of hand washing, Jesus told the Pharisees your worship is empty and worthless. He continued to say they failed to follow the instructions we received from the Creator because they loved their man-made traditions more than they love God. Are we any different today? There are some traditions in the modern churches that really don't cause any harm; that is until someone begins to believe the tradition becomes a command from Heaven.

8

***Behold, a virgin shall be with child, and
shall bring forth a son, and they shall call his
name Emmanuel, which being interpreted is,
God with us***

Matthew 1; 23 (King James)

WITH SUNDAY, EASTER and lent traditions lying in the garbage surely Christmas was still safe, the birth of the Messiah himself couldn't fall prey to pagan worship could it? What about the presents, the tree, the feeling of good will towards men, the Charlie Brown special even my favorite commercial growing up; Santa on that razor sledding across the snow? OK I stopped believing in Santa a long time ago but the thought of an old toymaker that only wants to make children smile isn't all bad is it? If you really want to keep your Christmas traditions and rituals you might want to skip this part but if you want to know what the Bible reveals about the birth of the Messiah and how we are to recognize him, stick with me.

December 25 on our calendar is just a few days after the winter solstice, this is a very special date to the pagans, and it seems every pagan sun god was born on the same day, what a coincidence. Well it really was not much of a coincidence, after the fall of the tower of Babel, and the confusion of language the same pagan worship followed each tribe as they went their own way. The names of the sun gods were changed by language but the rituals didn't change much. There was prayer, dancing, singing, child sacrifice, stuff like that. Wait a minute, child sacrifice? Yes it is where we get the name for Christmas, child mass, mass to sacrifice and "chris" child (not originally from the Greek Language.) Christos is a Greek word which means anointed or covered in oil, it was not the last name of the messiah. I had always been taught Christos meant god, seems I was misled. Child in Greek typically begins with "p-e-d-o" as in pediatrician child doctor or pedophile, no explanation needed.

Thou shalt not do so unto the Lord thy God: for every abomination to the Lord, which he hateth, have they done unto their gods; for even their sons and their daughters they have burnt in the fire to their gods Deuteronomy 12; 31 (King James) Here is where I need to give you the bad news, you might think we don't sacrifice our children in fire today but we do. We might not do it in any type of worship service yet, although it is done almost ritualistically. According to the experts in the field of bio-hazard waste, recommended and proper disposal of certain bio-hazard medical waste is incineration. Unfortunately, in this country an aborted fetus is considered bio-hazard medical waste. Yes Virginia (to steal a cliché') we do sacrifice our children in fire in the United States today.

Santa; say it ain't so! I really wish I could dismiss Santa as a fairy tale written for the pleasure of children. What began as a kind hearted old gentleman was twisted into an idle for the secular world to worship because once again we're much smarter than God. Now on Christmas morning children and adults alike kneel at the base of a tree worshiping presents in the presence of that phallic symbol to a pagan sun god, complete with the gold and silver balls, (use your imagination here) and we claim to be celebrating the birth of our savior.

I know what you're thinking, I said it too, "That's not what it means to me." The reality is; it doesn't matter what taking part in a pagan ceremony means to us, it matters what it means to God. When I first realized Christmas was a pagan celebration I was not expecting it. What could I do? I have Grandchildren to answer to for this. History again reared its ugly head and I learned that when this country was first settled, there was no Christmas so all of the cards and pictures you see with the pilgrims and a Christmas tree, didn't happen. In fact there were laws to prevent a business from being closed on December 25. Christmas was not a legal holiday until 1870, a result of the western European influence as more immigrants came to the United States. So when was Jesus born? The answer isn't from the lyrics of the songs we sing in church or from the Blind Boys from Alabama song, "the last Month of the Year." The answer is found in Scripture just like all of the other answers that really matter in this life.

What about the wise men and the manger? There was a manger and there were wise men but the only ones to come to the manger to see the new king were the shepherds. The wise men didn't show up until Y'shua, Jesus as we call him in English was older and living in a house. How many wise men were there? We don't know, scripture doesn't tell us but we know there were three gifts mentioned. Y'shua, the Hebrew pronunciation of who we call Jesus is named as the messiah in the Old Testament. When you read it in Hebrew, it makes perfect sense but Habakkuk and Jeremiah were not translated into English very well and it is confusing to read. I will be glad when I can read Hebrew better than I do now to improve my study time beyond the speed of a glacier. There was no "J" sound in Hebrew; Jesus didn't become a common name for Y'shua until about five hundred years ago. The "J" sound wasn't even used until the fourteenth century, seems something is trying to keep us from being able to use the real name of the messiah when we worship him.

So does this mean I shouldn't buy things from Thanksgiving until January? Of course not, take advantage of the sales, be a good steward of the blessings God gave you. Do not get caught up in the Christmas rush though, having to out-do last year, spend wisely. My wife loves Christmas music, it's festive, some habits are hard to break and quitting cold turkey might not be understood by family and friends but once they notice pagan celebrations not meaning anything to you, your excitement for the real Holidays will rub off. I'll admit tradition is hard to fight, even when it isn't about something important. I don't know how many times I've heard, "we've never done it that way before."

Most of my traditions were now just broken pieces of fluff, shredded piles of rituals were scattered in my brain. I had learned to worship in the pagan style since I was a child but now it was time to put that behind and learn what the Creator had intended. During this time I had discovered a Messianic fellowship and began to attend. They are a small group of believers who don't have or want an agenda other than to learn God's word and follow it as closely as they can. Other people began to reveal they had been secretly watching TV and internet sites that were devoted to Messianic fellowship. Some were like children with a new toy wanting to show everyone what they have found; others acted as if they were teenage boys who had just found a box of Playboy magazines. They would mention in conversation," I watched (insert show here) last night, did you see it?" Sometimes I had sometimes not, it didn't matter they would tell me all about it and I didn't mind hearing their commentary.

9

God is a Spirit: and they that worship him
must worship him in spirit and in truth
John 4; 24 (King James)

WITHIN THE PAGES of the Bible there are a lot of instructions for what not to do when it comes to worship. So how do we show our devotion to our creator? Leviticus 23 has opened my eyes to the wonder of God's Kingdom. Like most everyone else I was told the things in the Old Testament were Jewish and "we" didn't do those things. That is not what it reads, God said, "these are MY feasts." **_And the Lord spake unto Moses, saying, Speak unto the children of Israel, and say unto them, Concerning the feasts of the Lord, which ye shall proclaim to be holy convocations, even these are my feasts_**. Leviticus 23; 1–2 (King James)

He doesn't tell us they are Jewish or Methodist or Baptist, they belong to Him and they are to continue until he lets us know when we can stop. Right there in these verses the one true God, creator of Heaven and Earth reveals to us the way he wants to be worshiped. Contained in the celebrations of the feasts are the blueprint of who the Messiah is and how to recognize him. ***"For the law having a shadow of good things to come, and not the very image of the things, can never with those sacrifices which they offered year by year continually make the comers thereunto perfect."*** Hebrews 10; 1 (King James) Paul is telling us the feasts are shadow pictures, rehearsals so we are able to recognize the Messiah. These are to be practiced by us but completely satisfied by Y'shua.

John the disciple, who Jesus loved, uses the spring feasts in his gospel accounts to show the Hebrews how perfectly the life of the messiah mirrors what they have been practicing for over one thousand years. The people of that time were so caught up with the intricate details of keeping the feast they overlooked the big party. The one they had been waiting for was right there with them, teaching them, reminding them to keep the commandments that the Father had given to them and they missed it. The spring feast of Passover that had been done every year and only a small handful were able to receive the greatest blessing of having the prophet Moses said would come sitting with them. He ate with them, traveled with them, healed them and served them. Then he told them to go out and do all of that for someone else. The last hours of the life of our Messiah in his human form matches the Passover celebration in every detail, if you want to know how passionate Jesus was about carrying out the will of the father, celebrate the Passover and forget about a sunrise service that is basically meaningless except to Ra or Mithra (the Egyptian and Roman sun god)

Matthew's gospel in chapter 27 verses 52 and 53 refers to the tombs opening and the bodies of the saints appearing too many in the city. The second feast is the first fruit offering, Y'shua was gathering these first fruits when Mary came to the tomb and knowing she was there appeared to her. Y'shua had risen and was in the process of fulfilling the first fruit gathering when Mary came to the tomb. He appeared to her, sent her on her way, was able to take those first risen fruits to the Father and get back on the road to Emmaus with the two disciples just after lunch. We can only rehearse, the Messiah completes.

The fall feast are only partially complete, one of the names the Messiah is called is Emmanuel; God with us. God; able to enter into His creation and live or dwell with His people. The feast of Sukkot, or tabernacles, means just that; to live or dwell. Scripture tells us that Joseph went to Bethlehem to be counted in the census, why would Herod have people travel in the darkest part of the year to count the Jews when he knew that three times every year all Jewish men were required to be in one place? He wouldn't, the best time to count or control a crowd is when they are willingly in one place to celebrate and the romans were very good at crowd control.

Compare the birth of John the Baptist with the birth of his cousin Y'shua and we find another mathematical formula. Luke's account of the birth of the Messiah is detailed in such a way that every Hebrew who read it in the first century knew exactly what he meant. Change a couple of thousand years and add a different culture and you get the confusion we have today about this birthday. I choose not to offer the easy way here and lay out the entire answer. Hopefully if you have read this far, you will do what I did and seek conformation for yourself. You will look and find when the angel came to Zachariah and when he was in the temple. You will dig for the proof that I am wrong and that Christmas is Christmas after all. Then when you analyze the evidence that you have gathered and realize Y'shua was born in the fall of the year and not December 25, you will need to make a decision.

Who will you follow? Men who try to steal authority from God or the real Messiah who teaches us to do what Moses said to do. This Y'shua who was able to meet evil face to face in the desert and say, "It is written" Then allow the word of the creator to stand on its merits without adding anything or taking anything away. I can tell you from experience that this is not an easy choice. Family and friends think you have lost your mind but when you choose truth over tradition the thought of standing at the foot of the throne of grace isn't so scary. When the Creator judges me, if he asks any questions, I want to be able to say, "Ask your son, I tried to do what he said to do."

10

*And mount Sinai was altogether on a smoke,
because the Lord descended upon it in fire:
and the smoke thereof ascended as the
smoke of a furnace, and the whole mount
quaked greatly*
Exodus 19; 18

EVERYONE WHO WAS at the base of Mount Sinai heard the Creator as he shouted down the first Ten Commandments. They then begged Moses to ask God to stop and relay his message through him (Moses) so they didn't have to hear the voice of God any more. Moses went up the mountain and received the instructions that all of the people were to follow. As time passed God relayed through Moses a total of six hundred thirteen instructions, not all of these apply to every person. Some are for men, some for women, some for animals and some just for the Levite Priests. The Torah was read to the entire assembly at least once every seven years and was designed to be so easy to understand that a seven year old shepherd boy hearing it for the first time was expected to learn it.

People being people concentrate on the things we are told not to do and complain about the things we should do. That was true then and is still true today. Growing up, my mother would remind me to eat your peas, they're good for you. The Creator did the same when he told his chosen people what they should and shouldn't eat and that began with Adam and Eve. One of the first rules God had for his new creation concerned food.

And the Lord God commanded the man, saying, Of every tree of the garden thou mayest freely eat: But of the tree of the knowledge of good and evil, thou shalt not eat of it: for in the day that thou eatest thereof thou shalt surely die Genesis 2; 16–17 (King James) One simple rule and Eve couldn't get it, imagine her today trying to follow the American tax laws.

Dietary instructions are an important part of God's plan for us to be healthy and today we are living with the social and economic consequences of failing to follow his instruction. Obesity, diabetes and cancer are just the beginning of a long list of health issues which affect our lives and bank accounts. Science and medicine are just beginning to catch up to the reality of poor eating habits. For many years we have accepted certain food is good for us and now medical discoveries confirm certain foods cause health problems. Oceanography scientists now believe the heavy metals like mercury in fish can be attributed to the over fishing of shrimp and other shellfish which would normally clean up the water for the other species which swim in the water.

God had a plan for everything he created, shellfish filter the water and land animals like pigs are there to clean up dead animals just as some birds do. Gods menu did not include the animals intended to help clean his creation. Yea, I know I like a good bacon burger too and that is one of the most difficult for me to give up. Healthy minds and healthy bodies was the intention from the start and not just a recent advertising slogan. The creator really wants all of his children to live long healthy prosperous and productive lives and that is the reason he gave us the instructions about our food.

Want to feel better and live longer? Avoid the church ham and oyster dinners and follow the creators plan. Diet and exercise is what many doctors are telling their patients today, without knowing it what they are saying is, eat what is really good for you and obey the Sabbath. Here we are six thousand years after creation and science is finally catching up to God.

11

***I am the Lord thy God, which have brought
thee out of the land of Egypt, out of the house
of bondage***
Exodus 20; 2

WHEN THE HEBREWS were gathered at the base of
Mount Sinai, they heard the voice of God as He shouted
down the first instruction;

"***Thou shall have no gods before me***!" Exodus 20; 3
(King James)

A much better translation would be "You will not
put other gods in my face." That "before me" part of the
King James kept confusing my modern English, this isn't
a reference to a time period but a placement or priority.
Our Creator does not want us to be confused about who
He is; we are to have nothing to do with the worship of
false or pagan gods through ritual or tradition. God wants
us to worship Him the way He instructs us to, it pleases
Him when we try to do what He asks. We may not get
it completely correct all of the time but when our hearts
are in obeying He will be faithful and just to correct us

gently. When we are arrogant He will correct us harshly, either way God will be worshipped the way He wants to be worshipped. Each time Israel as a nation was defeated by an enemy or ejected from the land happened as a result of violating this first commandment. When they were faithful to the Torah, they enjoyed victory and peace. When they began mixing pagan worship together with the Torah or were worshipping other gods they were defeated in battle, removed from the land or both.

I have heard people say things such as, "well, that's the Old Testament" or "that was written for those people." I have to be careful when I hear these comments because I want to ask "Then why do you go to church?" In Matthew 5; 18 Y'shua is speaking, *for verily I say unto you, till Heaven and Earth pass, one* jot or one tittle shall in no wise pass from the law, till all be fulfilled." Matt. 5; 18 (King James)

What does that mean? Let's look at this carefully. Y'shua is saying truly, for certain, as long as Heaven and earth remain not the smallest letter either vowel or consonant will God allow to be changed in His instructions. Has Earth passed? Not yet and Heaven has not either! So the Old Testament that was written for those people is still enforced for us today in Heaven and on Earth!

John 14 Y'shua again is teaching,

> *"And I will do whatever you ask in my name, so that the Father may be glorified in the Son. You may ask me for anything in my name, and I will do it. If you love me, keep my commands. And I will ask the Father, and he will give you another advocate to help you and be with you forever."* John 14; 13–16 (NIV)

Why did he stop in the middle and say, "if you love me keep my commands." And what are the commands of the Messiah? These go farther than the love the LORD your God and love your neighbor. Y'shua is getting at the heart of the Torah, If you love the son, do what he said to do, follow the instructions the Father gave us and you will be on solid spiritual ground to ask for the things which will glorify the father. In other words, when you follow the instructions you will know what to ask for and how to ask so that whatever you ask will be given to you. When we are standing on that solid ground we will not be under the influence of pagan gods or performing pagan rituals, we will be worshipping God the way He intends for us to worship Him and only Him.

Are you still not willing to give up those pagan traditions? Let's go to Revelation. Many people think this last book of the Bible is the revelation of the apostle John, and they would be mistaken. The first verse of the first chapter begins, "The revelation of Jesus Christ," which makes this the revelation of the Messiah and not John. Why the confusion? Many Bibles have the book titled "The revelation of St. John the Devine," which is in itself misguiding. John at this point in his life was exiled on the island of Patmos; he had been persecuted, beaten and according to some boiled alive in oil for preaching the death and resurrection of Y'shua. He never gave up and his persistence was rewarded with a visit by none other than the Messiah himself, alive and well in his glorified body which John describes. Then Y'shua gives John the job of taking dictation, telling him to write down what he has seen, what he sees now and what he will be told to write in the future.

John diligently writes what he is shown, Y'shua walking among the assemblies in Asia Minor, watching their actions and then he tells john to write to the churches. These letters are not to be taken lightly, there are some disturbing actions these churches have been doing and they are getting a literal "come to Jesus" moment. Of all the letters the third written to the church in Sardis beginning with chapter 3 stands out. Y'shua tells them he knows their works (what they have been doing) he knows they have made a name for themselves in the community and they are dead.

"And unto the angel of the church in Sardis write; These things saith he that hath the seven Spirits of God, and the seven stars; I know thy works, that thou hast a name that thou livest, and art dead." (Revelation 3; 1 (King James) These are hard words coming from the king of love, especially if we compare the actions of our churches today with that of Sardis. He goes on to tell them he had not found their works perfect before (in His presence) God and they need to get their act together before (time-wise) it is too late. Then he gives some encouragement, there are some but just a few who are holding on to the instructions. They will be walking with the Messiah, they are getting themselves cleaned up and ready, they didn't stay in the sin where they were when Y'shua heard their cry.

The church in Sardis is a great example of "all are called but few choose to follow." Everybody wants to go to Heaven but very few are willing to do what it takes to get there. For too many years we have been told that all we need to do is have faith, that is a wonderful start but we can not simply have faith and then continue a lifestyle in which our actions show we are spiritually dead. When we choose to stay where we were when we met the Messiah shows no willingness to change on our part. Remember we are the ones who must change our actions, He is the role model, we need to be more like Y'shua and not try to make him more like us.

God isn't just a free 911 call, He will make his presence known when you call out because he is always with you but then we need to react. That please God throw me a rope line implies you intend to catch it and hold on. Too many people today think that because we have this thing called grace we don't need to follow the instructions, we don't need to walk down the narrow path; grace is what gives us the strength and courage to do those things. Grace is not an invisible rope that we can tie on to our lives and expect God to be a tugboat and us the barge. We are expected to continue under our own power, the Messiah sets the course, grace is the fuel and God will make sure we never run out. Just as our physical bodies will always accept sugar into the cells and turn that sugar into energy so we can work or play; grace is the spiritual sugar God provides which gives us the energy and courage to live our lives according to His instructions. We should not abuse grace the way Jude describes, grace is not a license to sin;

"For certain individuals whose condemnation was written about long ago have secretly slipped in among you. They are ungodly people, who pervert the grace of our God into a license for immorality and deny Jesus Christ our only Sovereign and Lord." Jude 1; 4 (NIV)

There is a prosperity gospel being taught in our churches today that describes this verse. All you have to do to get into Heaven is say this little prayer, accept Jesus into your heart and your passport to heaven is stamped, as long as you keep writing the church a check every week. Who prospers from this? The church does. Years ago there was a famous preacher on television who claimed that salvation is free. He was almost right, you can't buy your way into Heaven but it isn't free, it costs change. Repentance, change in lifestyle, you can't continue in sin and expect to walk through the pearly gates.

Like John never give up, stay persistent to follow the instructions and you will be rewarded. Nobody ever said it would be easy but they said it would be worthwhile. Be careful not to be like the church in Sardis, don't allow your actions to make you look like you're dead, I can't think of a criticism more harsh from the Messiah than that unless it would be "who are you and what are you doing here."

12

Why do thy disciples transgress the tradition of the elders? for they wash not their hands when they eat bread. But he answered and said unto them, Why do ye also transgress the commandment of God by your tradition?
Matthew 15; 2–3 (King James)

THE TRADITIONS MANY of us grew up with took many years to become so entrenched in our minds that today we think of them as scripture. I have seen cards with the babe in a manger next to a tree with lights and ornaments. I have seen pictures of Jesus as a clean cut young man carrying his Bible to Sunday school. I was taught the Sunday school song about "only a boy named David, only a little sling." But when we really begin to dig into the word of the Creator we get a more clear picture, no tree or wise men at the manger, certainly no Sunday school for Y'shua and David was fully grown when he defeated that giant. The clothing we expect to see on biblical performers is only a Hollywood image in most cases and although he had a wonderful voice, Charlton Heston was not Moses.

Many centuries of lies have turned valuable life lessons into mere stories, and we wonder why there is the social decline in the world today. Every denomination is trying to make some kind of change that will bring people back to church. Here is a radical idea, teach the truth! Forget about "religion" tell people the plain truth, God is alive and well and so is the son. No, you don't have to be a Methodist or Baptist or any other denomination to get into Heaven but you do have to believe that God is the Creator of the universe and He sent the Messiah to purchase our contract of death with His blood and then follow the instructions.

Because I choose to believe the whole Bible and try to follow the Torah I have been asked when did you convert to being Jewish? That depends on your definition of Jewish; having an ancestry which traces back to Abraham makes one a Jew (Judean) or Hebrew by birth. Since I have such a mixed up ancestry I don't know if I can claim that birthright. Modern Judaism is a religion, a man made religion which attempts to control every aspect of your life including which shoe to put on first in the morning. So the answer is no, I don't practice Judaism, Methodism or any other man made religious system. I simply attempt to follow the instructions found in the first five books of the bible, then learn from the lessons in the rest of it. I am amazed at how simple it is not to be bothered with religious thinking and be free to concentrate on what the Creator wants from me.

My father had a sign in his workshop that read,"when all else fails, read the instructions." Truer words may have never been spoken. The whole time I thought something was missing in my life, the instructions were there but I wasn't ready to follow them, I had to try it my way. When I couldn't figure out the code in the Bible, there wasn't one; I just wouldn't give up my traditional way of thinking. Not until I was ready to listen to the Creator, would he show me what I needed to see because I had been too busy looking for what I wanted to see.

Some traditions are great, like fireworks on July 4, or birthday cake. Some traditions are a wedge that satan tries to drive between the Creator and the created like weeping for Tammuz or Christmas. We have the freedom to choose which we follow and where we wind up when the last trumpet sounds. The choice is yours to make, nobody can pray anyone else into Heaven, your decisions and your actions are your responsibility. God doesn't just want to hear you love Him, God wants to see you love Him. The question is, Are you ready and willing to give up tradition for truth?

What about the other traditions we have learned to follow? Y'shua saved a wonderful teaching for the last night he spent with his disciples before the crucifixion. This "last supper" has been reduced to a convenient ritual we call communion. Too many in the Christian Church are under the false belief that the "last supper" was a Passover Seder meal. This comes from misunderstanding of Luke 22 and possibly another mistranslation as well. There are no supporting passages in scripture which give credence for the "last supper" to be anything other than a regular meal. There are however passages which affirm the Passover was the next evening, let's examine them.

"Jesus answered, He it is, to whom I shall give a sop, when I have dipped it. And when he had dipped the sop, he gave it to Judas Iscariot, the son of Simon. And after the sop Satan entered into him. Then said Jesus unto him, That thou doest, do quickly. Now no man at the table knew for what intent he spake this unto him. For some of them thought, because Judas had the bag, that Jesus had said unto him, Buy those things that we have need of

against the feast; or, that he should give something to the poor. He then having received the sop went immediately out: and it was night" John 13; 26–30 (King James)

In these passages we read clearly that the disciples thought that Judas was going out to make a purchase or to give money to the poor, neither could have been done if this were Passover, a High Sabbath. There would not have been any place Judas could go to buy anything and no Israeli, no matter how poor would have taken money on a Sabbath day.

Another discredit to the "last supper" being a Passover Seder is also found in John. *"Then led they Jesus from Caiaphas unto the hall of judgment: and it was early; and they themselves went not into the judgment hall, lest they should be defiled; but that they might eat the Passover"* John 18; 28 (King James) The Pharisees take Y'shua back to Pilate's judgment hall but only Y'shua went in, the Pharisees stayed outside so they would remain able to eat the Passover!

There are other non-scriptural yet cultural reasons for the "last supper" not being a Seder which would be far too cumbersome to include here. The teaching Y'shua offers about the bread reach far back to Abraham as he declares that today you will witness a promise made to Abraham by the Father is kept. The wine is a witness that Y'shua is able to renew the blood covenant made at Mount Sanai which we violated. Y'shua's blood buys the contract for our brokenness and our unfaithfulness. Still we have Y'shua's promise that if we stay faithful and do our best to follow the Torah, the instructions from the Creator, we will be present to see him raise a cup once again. Yes this teaching reaches from Abraham to Revelation and still most only want to see a ten minute fantasy.

"Cursed is anyone who does not uphold the
words of this law by carrying them out."
Then all the people shall say, "Amen!"
Deuteronomy 27; 26 (NIV)

THERE DO YOU begin? Right now, make a conscious decision to follow the instructions we are given in the Bible then ask the King of the Universe to help you on your way. I can guarantee this will not be an easy journey, look no further than the book of Job and you will learn that trusting in God is a two way street. When we place our faith and trust in Him, He in turn wants to trust us as well, why else would God offer Job to be tested by satan? ***And the Lord said unto Satan, Hast thou considered my servant Job, that there is none like him in the earth, a perfect and an upright man, one that feareth God, and escheweth evil?*** Job 1; 8 (King James)

Job trusted God and God trusted Job enough to offer satan the chance to try and get Job to give up that trust. No matter what satan tried, no matter how often satan went to God to ask permission to make life even more miserable,

Job remained faithful and trusted that God had a reason for allowing satan to influence his life.

Remember satan has some limited authority in this world, satan is not in control over this world!

GOD REMAINS IN COMPLETE CONTROL OVER HEAVEN AND EARTH!

Have you ever asked the question "Why do bad things happen to good people?" The answer is in how we respond, when we react as if even the bad things we may be called to endure is God trusting us to show others our faith, others will notice how strong our faith really is. An older gentleman I knew found out he had cancer, during one of our conversations he asked, "I have been going to church all of my life, why would God punish me at this age?" After I explained he wasn't being punished but he was being trusted to show others how to remain faithful when we are going through a bad time he had a mild change of attitude. He always wanted to make people think he was a rough tough old codger but anyone who would take a few minutes to get to know him knew his faith was unshakeable and he was faithful until he passed. The last chance I had to see him was in the hospital about a week before he died, we both knew he didn't have much time left but his spirits were good and he did say there were times when he wondered if God knew what he was doing through his illness. He may never know how much his remaining true to the creator strengthened my faith so when I see him again I will be sure to tell him. Yes it is OK to question God, if we don't ask, how else will we be able to get answers? We might not like the answers we receive but we remain faithful and trust that God gives us what we need and not always what we want.

Why trust God when He allows us to face challenges? Have you ever watched a team work? Whether a ball team or a team of horses or oxen, when things are tough they pull together to accomplish what needs to be done. One person can't win a football game by their self and one horse can't do the job of two or more. When you begin living like Y'shua is right by your side ready to help with the easy things as well as the hard stuff, you are on a team that will never lose because when Y'shua is on your team everything will be done for the glory of the father. Nobody ever promised things would be easy, anything worthwhile seldom is easy but when we reach our goals all the garbage we had to put up with is forgotten. Job remained faithful and was blessed abundantly for his faith, he had some trouble along the way but he knew when everything was over how much God trusted him and how much God loved him.

The second step to be free of the pagan junk is to recognize it for what it is; trash to be thrown out. Traditions based in pagan rituals are everywhere; question them, ask where to find it in scripture. Don't worry about offending someone or putting them on the spot (at the right time of course) you have an obligation to know the truth about why you worship the way you do. I was in a Bible study one morning when someone asked a question about the Sabbath. The preacher quickly responded "my Sabbath is on Friday!" OK he is the preacher and the one leading the study, after it was over I went and asked him if he understood the meaning of the Sabbath rest and the lessons we learned from the Manna which God provided to the Israelites in the desert, he didn't. All he knew was what he had been taught by our fathers who have inherited lies. He never questioned their teaching and to make things worse he perpetuated the lies he inherited. He was also unwilling to read the scripture for himself to find out if what I was saying was wrong or right, I welcome a debate from these mindless pulpit puppets, they are easy to leave disillusioned and empty. Preachers like this are the ones Y'shua was speaking about false teaching;

But whoso shall offend one of these little ones which believe in me, it were better for him that a millstone were hanged about his neck, and that he were drowned in the depth of the sea." Matthew 18; 6 (King James)

Y'shua does not take false teaching lightly. Careful study of the scripture in the correct context will allow you to hear when the word of the creator has been twisted.

Make the decision to be more than a pew warmer, God is available all of the time. Yes it takes work to be more than cannon fodder for satan and you should want to be more than that. Some people go through life without any idea of who or where they are, you see them all the time; those folks in the store who stand and stare aimlessly into space with no clue about anything or anyone around them.

"These are spots in your feasts of charity, when they feast with you, feeding themselves without fear: clouds they are without water, carried about of winds; trees whose fruit withereth, without fruit, twice dead, plucked up by the roots;

Raging waves of the sea, foaming out their own shame; wandering stars, to whom is reserved the blackness of darkness for ever." Jude 1; 12–13 (King James)

Commit yourself to at least 30 minutes of study each day, yes it is difficult at first but after about a month if you're faithful you look forward to it. Don't be afraid to become a pastor's nightmare, when you can question a sermon topic and show in scripture his triumphs and errors he will respect you even if he won't see Heaven for the pagan traditions. True disciples of the Messiah will learn quickly to recognize certain keywords and phrases from religious agendas and unfortunately there are many in the world. The easiest to spot concern money, when you hear about stewardship and finance mentioned more than ten times in a twenty minute sermon keep your hand on your wallet and don't take it out of your pocket. About once or twice each year it may be necessary to spend more time speaking about finances but not every week through the entire message. Every ministry asks for donations, be a good steward of your finances and give wisely to the ministry which you care about the most.

During one service the Pastor made several suggestions that there were things in the Bible that were outdated and needed to be thrown out. Afterward when I was offering my displeasure to one of the congregates, he made the comment that we need to listen with an open heart even when we don't agree with what is being said. I answered that we do need to have an open heart when we hear someone twisting the word of God but that does not mean we must give up what scripture tells us and march behind a false teacher straight through the gates into hell! Call false teaching what it is and follow the Messiah; he is the way, the truth and the light. When these false teachers speak don't be willing to follow them because they have some degree or spent time in Seminary. Scrutinize what they say using scripture, if they don't twist it to fit their agenda and they uphold who Y'shua is then you will know the character of their heart.

Are you ready to find others, who want to give up their pagan traditions, throw out the garbage and follow the instructions? This might be easier than you thought. I have been to many congregations through the years and have met a lot of people who have the same desire. Begin by asking, then when you have a few interested people start a study group. Before long you will have an assembly and can begin to share the celebration feasts together. Be cautious not to get caught in the religious traps of man-made traditions. Don't allow yourself to teach tradition as scripture or to use scripture out of context to make your tradition fit what you want just because you like it. I have taken part in many very nice Christmas and Easter services (before I knew the truth) which many thought were uplifting and wonderful but other than for the sake of tradition these services were the "clanging gongs" Paul writes about. Even when we were trying to uphold and glorify Jesus these services were empty because they didn't conform to Deuteronomy 12; 4

***"Do not worship the LORD your God in their* {pagan}** *way"* Deut. 12; 4 (NIV with addition)

This doesn't mean that God wouldn't use these services to change the heart of someone and wake up that spirit inside of them but it wasn't showing them the one true God for who He really is.

*But if the wicked will turn from all his sins
that he hath committed, and keep all my
statutes, and do that which is lawful and
right, he shall surely live, he shall not die.
All his transgressions that he hath committed,
they shall not be mentioned unto him: in his
righteousness that he hath done he shall live*
Ezekiel 18; 21–22 (King James)

THROUGH THE YEARS I have heard many people express what sin is to them, going to the movies, dancing, drinking alcohol, smoking and many more. Sin is what separates us from God, sin is the wedge that satan tries to drive between our spirit and the Holy Spirit. These are the results of sin. Sure we humans do many things that are not healthy for us but John defined sin in his first letter this way;

"Everyone who sins breaks the law; in fact, sin is lawlessness." 1 John 3; 4 (NIV)

So according to John, sin is not following the instructions God gave to us through Moses! How many times have you heard that in a Sunday morning sermon? Even some of the Rabbinical Messianic assemblies don't teach this because they enjoy their traditions that don't follow the Torah.

For me this was a whack in the back of the head moment that makes you stand up and take notice. When all of the traditions I had been taught since I was a child were still confetti swirling in the air now I learn sin is failing to follow the instructions. That made me a multiple offender with a "rap sheet" longer than anyone could imagine and there was no comfort in knowing I was not alone. There was comfort in asking for forgiveness and help to learn how to worship the way God wants to be worshipped. When that happened, I lost the feeling that something was missing, that was replaced by a new understanding of who God is and who the Messiah is. Finally, I was able to understand that Y'shua came to be that perfect example for us to follow because he never once violated the Torah. Jesus was able to live his life on this earth without giving in to the influential desires the world offers. The Messiah, the prophet Moses spoke of that we must hear and obey, our high priest forever, the only son of God embraced the instructions both in spirit and in this physical world.

Did Y'shua set such a high standard that we have no hope to achieve it? Not really, we humans simply refuse to believe that living the way our Creator intended is not complicated. The entire Torah was to be read to everyone living with the Nation of Israel every seven years, so a child hearing it for the first time was expected to understand it. This same child should have been able to learn by being surrounded by others who were obeying the instructions. Here is the big BUT; even shortly after we had the instructions, we thought we could improve them. When the Messiah came, he told us the Torah was already the way

God wanted it, there was no need to try and improve it, just do it. When Y'shua was dressing down the Pharisees he said this;

"For they bind heavy burdens and grievous to be borne, and lay them on men's shoulders; but they themselves will not move them with one of their fingers." Matthew 23; 4 (King James)

These heavy burdens and grievous' are all of the extra garbage we have added to the instructions. Think of it this way instead of inserting tab A into slot B; we thought it would be better to glue a certain measure on to tab A and then somehow close up slot B before we try to make them fit together. Again Jesus tells us not to live by the things that were added to the instructions but live according to the instructions. He was telling us over and over that if we live by the Torah we would not be living in sin.

I know many very nice people who go to church every week and freely give their tithes and offerings and believe they are saved but they continue to live in sin because in their mind the Old Testament was only for the Jews. The Apostle Paul tells us if we put our faith in the Creator and believe that Y'shua (Jesus) came to save us then we are grafted into the children of God.

"If some of the branches have been broken off, and you, though a wild olive shoot, have been grafted in among the others and now share in the nourishing sap from the olive root." Romans 11; 17 (NIV)

We share equally with the chosen children of God, I was that wild olive and if you want to think about it another way;

"For ye have not received the spirit of bondage again to fear; but ye have received the Spirit of adoption, whereby we cry, Abba, Father." Romans 8; 15 (King James)

We have been adopted by our creator and he wants to be our father, the one who cares for us. To accept Y'shua into your life means you accept the rest of the family also. We may not always agree on everything just like any family but with our faith and trust in our creator we have one common goal and that is to do what the Messiah tells us we should do, obey the commands of the father.

15

But Jonah rose up to flee unto Tarshish from the presence of the Lord, and went down to Joppa; and he found a ship going to Tarshish: so he paid the fare thereof, and went down into it, to go with them unto Tarshish from the presence of the Lord
Jonah 1; 3

IF YOU ARE still reading this either from curiosity, anger, frustration or boredom, whether you realize this or not; you have that spirit in you trying to connect to the Holy Spirit of the creator. When I began my journey, I had no idea where it would take me. There were times I thought I was driving but I was only along for the ride. I never expected to know as much about the creator, the Messiah, religions or tradition as I have learned and there is so much more to learn.

When God spoke and created this universe we live in, He began a series of events that we have been trying to understand since Adam took his first breath and opened his eyes. That feeling of awe and having such a close connection to God must have been exciting. Imagine holding a conversation with the Creator much like visiting with a friend in your home. That is the relationship God wants with us now and He has offered us the way to have it if we want it.

Yes God knows some will turn their back on Him;

"But, dear friends, remember what the apostles of our Lord Jesus Christ foretold. They said to you, "In the last times there will be scoffers who will follow their own ungodly desires." These are the people who divide you, who follow mere natural instincts and do not have the Spirit." Jude 1; 17–19 (NIV)

These people will never know the excitement or joy of a relationship with the Messiah and will not understand why they will suffer an eternity of torture. These are the people who are led by lies, do evil things and create chaos. Yes they will suffer for refusing to hear the truth but it is their choice to make and God loves them enough to allow them to choose. Our ambition should be to spread the good news of salvation through the Messiah to as many as we can while realizing we will not be able to reach every heart.

Paul put it kind of like this; run the race, fight the good fight, it's worth it! Don't give up now and lose all you have been given so far. When I found out some of the things I had been taught were lies it did take the wind out of my sails. Surrendering to the world never crossed my mind, if I had been misguided by well-meaning pastors and friends then I needed to know why. This journey is still no vacation, there are still very good friends who can't understand why I would leave a worship community that is full of compassion and good works to follow the real Y'shua. I don't expect them or anyone else to immediately turn their life around on a dime; this took me years of study to find the truth. Hopefully little by little, those of us who have found the Bible to be true from the first word of Genesis to the last Amen of Revelation will be able to express the truth to those who have ears to hear. We will try to introduce them to the real Y'shua and to the creator, the God of Abraham, Isaac and Jacob for those who have the eyes to see. One person at a time will know their religious traditions are worthless in the eyes of God and begin to follow His instructions. Then on the day that Y'shua returns, when the sky splits open and he sends his angels to gather the saints, we will feast with him and hear him say, "Well done good and faithful servants." And that will only be the beginning.

Portions of pagan sun god rituals have found their way into every religious system in the world today. These rituals do not discriminate between Christian, Judaism, Islam, Hinduism or any other of the thousands of religions that are practiced by well-intentioned although misinformed worshippers. Satan desires nothing more than to spread his lies to prevent all of us from being able to follow the instructions we were given by our creator. Far too many of us have accepted the lies which we have inherited from our ancestors but there is hope.

Imagine, reading your Bible without any pre-conceived ideas or agendas. Actually reading what is there and hearing directly from Heaven without the influence of worldly men. There is no code in the Bible which hides who God is and how He intends for us to live, there is only our prejudices based on the lies we have inherited. We must break through the hard shell of those lies to get to the true word of God, test everything, including what I have written and then keep what is good. This is the generation that has all of the information, archeological evidence and tools that allows us to contend for the Gospel which was once delivered to the saints.

The question is; are you willing to put your traditions, your doctrines of men, to that test, or are you too comfortable where you are?

SUMMARY

Amen

IF WE CHOOSE to believe the Bible in its completeness, when John writes that sin is the failure to follow the instructions given to us through Moses by the Creator, we must examine ourselves. Are we living according to Scripture or just following our religious doctrine and traditions that often require us to sin in the face of God. Our prayer needs to be for God to teach us to see things the way He does; that we learn to love what He loves and despise what He says is an abomination.

For too many years we have leaned on misinformation and excuses such as, we are only human or we live in a broken world. If being mortal was an acceptable excuse, why expel Adam and Eve out of the garden? I can imagine that conversation; "But we're only human" they would cry in a whiny voice. The answer, yes you are only human and you are created with the ability to know and do better. Because God has given us His breath of life we lowly humans are above the animals which were only given life without the Spirit of God. Our Creator has given us the gift of connection to Him. Without being able to connect, we would simply go through life being unaware of how great and wonderful this life is. Can a wild animal look at the sunrise, the stars or even its surroundings and begin to appreciate any of these things? No, the animals we share this world with do not have the breath of God's Spirit in them, we do.

The farther we are from creation the less familiar we are with the Creator and how His creation works. The pyramids were built a few thousand years ago and with all of our technology today we can't build anything to those same specifications. We simply forgot how the Creator intended the universe to work and unfortunately, we have forgotten how to remain connected to the Creator. He chose to give us His instructions concerning how we are to have long healthy lives and we refuse to follow His instructions. There is hope and there is a choice.

When we choose to read the Bible as it was written, not trying to twist it to make it fit our ideas but being willing to change ourselves to conform to God's instructions, then we are off to a good start. Remember even satan has faith in God, there is a transcript of a conversation between satan and the Creator in the first chapter of Job. Satan knows who God is and he still tries to twist God's words to suit his purpose. Our choice should not be to follow satan's example but to follow the Messiah's example. Don't try to make God fit into what we want Him to fit into; try to make ourselves fit into what God wants us to be. God created us for a reason and He wants us to know Him as a child knows a parent. The choice is yours to make, will you believe the words of the Creator, the Messiah, the prophets and the Apostles, or will you deny them and continue putting your faith in the empty traditions of pagan worship and the worthless doctrines on men? Whichever you choose, whatever choice you make, eternity is a very long time to remember the consequences of your decision. I hope you would choose to spend eternity in the presence of the Messiah, learning as much as we can about the Creator while in the comfort of the Holy City John saw in his vision. You are free to choose the lake of fire with endless suffering and torment, wondering how and where you went wrong. Choose carefully and may the Holy Spirit guide you and the words of Yehovah comfort you as you study the Scriptures to find what the Creator is revealing to you.

DOES ANYONE KNOW THE WAY TO MOUNT SINAI?

MANY PREACHERS HAVE attempted to convince sinners to repent by comparing the Hebrew bondage in Egypt with our slavery to sin. They stand in their pulpits and tell their congregations that just as God led those slaves out of Egypt He will lead you out of your sin. While that is basically true, there is far more meaning to the lessons of the Exodus than simply being someplace other than where you were. Pastors charm their parishioners and tickle their ears with the words they want to hear. 2 Timothy 4; 3–4

For the time will come when they will not endure sound doctrine; but after their own lusts shall they heap to themselves teachers, having itching ears; And they shall turn away their ears from the truth, and shall be turned unto fables (KJV)

The mantra of the modern Christian church has become "just accept Jesus into your heart, that's all you need to do." Unfortunately the pastor's job has changed from being a shepherd for his flock to "fleecing" the sheep. Thankfully not all churches are this way, there are some churches in the world that are more concerned with your soul than your checkbook and if you have found one of them consider yourself very blessed. So how did the modern church move from "go and sin no more" to "all you need is faith?" to understand that let's go back to Genesis.

Joseph, while in Egypt had the opportunity to learn many lessons and he learned them well. Being handpicked by the Pharaoh to make sure Egypt had the provisions needed to survive a seven year famine was a tremendous responsibility. Having your estranged family invited to live in the best part of the country by Pharaoh added to what Joseph must have thought was a burden. Having survived the famine and family reunion, the sons of Jacob remained in Egypt, they had many, many children and as time passed they began to think of the land as belonging to them. The Hebrew children forgot that they were invited to live in Egypt and likewise the Egyptians forgot about everything that Joseph had done for them. This was a cultural time bomb and to put what was happening into today's language; the Hebrews had worn out their welcome.

A new Pharaoh, who didn't learn history, looked at a group of people that he thought were going to be trouble. Pharaoh began to speak out against the Hebrews to convince the rest of Egypt to enslave them. Exodus 1; 9–10

And he said unto his people, Behold, the people of the children of Israel are more and mightier than we: Come on, let us deal wisely with them; lest they multiply, and it come to pass, that, when there falleth out any war, they join also unto our enemies, and fight against us, and so get them up out of the land. (KJV)

Pharaoh in verse 9 uses the argument that the Hebrew people were mightier than Egypt and wanted to deal wisely with them and continues in verse 10 they might defeat Egypt and then leave. Obviously Pharaoh, was looking for a way to keep the Hebrews in Egypt, he didn't want them leaving but he did want complete control over them. Pharaoh realized the Hebrew people were a valuable commodity to Egypt and he needed them to remain to build a stronger nation, the problem was he wanted them to become Egyptian and forget about Abraham and his strange God. Pharaoh's plan was to enslave the Hebrew people, Exodus 1; 11

Therefore they did set over them taskmasters to afflict them with their burdens. And they built for Pharaoh treasure cities, Pithom and Raamses. (KJV)

While we are not told in scripture exactly how the people we made slaves, we know their work was not easy, Exodus 1; 13–14

And the Egyptians made the children of Israel to serve with rigour: And they made their lives bitter with hard bondage, in morter, and in brick, and in all manner of service in the field: all their service, wherein they made them serve, was with rigour. (KJV)

Finally when the Egyptians thought they were in complete control they began to systematically extinguish what they thought was any hope of continuing to be a separate people. Exodus 1; 16

And he said, When ye do the office of a midwife to the Hebrew women, and see them upon the stools; if it be a son, then ye shall kill him: but if it be a daughter, then she shall live. (KJV)

By killing the male children the females would eventually be forced to marry Egyptian men and the children of

Abraham would be exterminated. Of course that also meant that the free labor force would need to be replaced as well but pharaoh would resolve that issue when he needed to.

Finally things were going so poorly for the Hebrew children they began to remember, they remembered Abraham and his God and they cried out to Him. God already had planned to bring them out of Egypt; He had people in the right places to do the things that were necessary to get them out of their slavery. Moses, the one who was born to be raised in Pharaoh's home, learn how he thought and be familiar enough to speak directly to pharaoh. Most people read the account of the burning bush as god simply giving orders to Moses but it was the ultimate job interview. Moses would still be a shepherd but not for Jethro, although he tried to convince God that he was not the right man for the mission God knew he could depend on Moses. God wasn't worried that Moses didn't think he was good enough, couldn't speak well enough and God wasn't worried about Pharaoh wanting to kill Moses either because He had put each person in the place that they needed to be so the people could get out of Slavery.

The lessons of the Exodus from Egypt are more than just being brought out of the land, each piece had to be placed properly for God's plan to work. Things are the same today, when we are proud, selfish, arrogant, greedy, depressed, and sick and the list goes on; we enslave ourselves voluntarily to sin. Just like Pharaoh, satan doesn't want us to escape; he needs that free labor force to work for him. Satan works at exterminating the people we were and tries to force us to become someone else. Thankfully, God has put the people in place to lead us out of our slavery, they may not be who you think they are, they might not work miracles but they are there, right where you need them. These are the people who are nurses and doctors on the rehab centers; they are the financial advisors who offer free service to the poor. They volunteer at shelters and thrift stores and they are your fathers, sons, mothers, daughters, husband and wives. They are the ones who are brave enough to hold your hand, listen to your trouble and will let you stay in a jail cell if that is where you need to be at that time. The one thing each of these people has in common is they know Yeshua, (Jesus) and they trust Him to guide them to do what needs to be done to break the chains that hold someone in the bondage of sin. Just like Moses lead the people through the red sea and on to meet God at Mount Sinai, these people can introduce you to the Messiah and He is willing to lead you as well.

Today too many preachers and other good church people stop the story right there, they forget what happens next. There are more lessons to be learned; just because you are able to leave a bad situation doesn't mean you have what you need to live in the world. Yehovah didn't abandon the Hebrew people in the desert, He gave them water, food and much more; He taught them how to live. Moses brought the people to Mount Sanai, Yehovah told Moses to ask this question, Exodus 19; 4–6

Ye have seen what I did unto the Egyptians, and how I bare you on eagles' wings, and brought you unto myself. Now therefore, if ye will obey my voice indeed, and keep my covenant, then ye shall be a peculiar treasure unto me above all people: for all the earth is mine: And ye shall be unto me a kingdom of priests, and an holy nation. These are the words which thou shalt speak unto the children of Israel. (KJV)

God wanted to know if the mixed multitude (the Hebrew children and the others that joined with them) would be willing to be His people. They didn't know what the instructions would be but they knew He had freed them from their slavery, they knew this God had taken them out of a bad situation so of course they said "YES!"

Today we know what the instructions are, we have them written down for us in one convenient book but people try to avoid them. We have the instructions from our Creator letting us know how we are to live once we have been set free. We have the opportunity to read them and understand them before we say "yes," we are given the chance to reject Yehovah, His plans and the people He put in place to free us and many people do reject that. Unfortunately, many preachers teach that we no longer need God's instructions, we just need to believe. They will tell us the law has been fulfilled but they can't show us in Scripture where to find that because it isn't there. They will preach from the pulpit that those who obey the God's law are under a curse because they don't want to live their own lives the way our Creator designed them to live. They are still in the chains of sin, bound to satan's workforce by demonic overseers. They are the ones we are warned about by Yeshua Himself, Matthew 24; 5

For many shall come in my name, saying, I am Christ; and shall deceive many. (KJV)

We are told that many will proclaim Yeshua as Messiah but they will lead you away from Him and into slavery. James 2; 19

Thou believest that there is one God; thou doest well: the devils also believe, and tremble. (KJV)

Satan knows Yehovah, In Job there is a transcription of a conversation between the two. Having faith or believing is only the beginning; acting on that faith is where the real freedom begins. When we want something to eat we need to take some physical action to eat. When we want out of a bad situation simply thinking about it won't change where we are. Yehovah has those people in place to get us out of slavery and just like the Hebrew people followed Moses, we should follow them. Yes when you're in the desert you might want to go back, there are some bridges we need to burn and watch fall into the river that separates the past from the present. Use the resources provided to move forward not back. It's time to stop working in the forced labor camp of sin and be free.

Some people want to proclaim that following our Creators instructions is "legalism." The first response to that should be why wouldn't you do the things Yehovah wants you to do? Why would you want to live in a way you were not designed to live? And finally, if following God's instructions is legalistic does that mean that being rebellious and not obeying God is illegalistic?

Failing to follow God's instructions at Mount Sinai didn't work well for the people that were there, remember the golden calf incident. Yehovah told them "no idols" so they made one anyway. Since they used an animal as an idol, God chose to have them sacrifice animals as a constant reminder they had broken a blood covenant. They would keep that service in place until the perfect lamb was sacrificed and the price that we could never afford was paid by Yeshua.

The lessons we learn from the Exodus are important today, our Creator set a precedent for our benefit and too many people want to dismiss these lessons as being outdated. From the feast days that were established in Genesis to the way we treat our Creator and each other we learned about at Mount Sinai. From living as a slave in Egypt or a slave to sin, His instructions were given teaching us how to live in freedom at Mount Sinai. The Torah, the word of Yehovah, His word of life was given to us at Mount Sinai. Shouldn't you learn the way to Mount Sinai?

THIS PLACE
CALLED HEAVEN

THERE ARE SO many commentaries and so much speculation about what is written in the Bible that far too many people will not actually read what is written but wonders why there seems to be conflicts within the pages of Scripture. Careful study reveals there are no conflicts in the Bible, the conflicts rest squarely on the shoulders of the people who twist the words of God and try to make them fit into our agenda, our idea of how we think the universe should work. Of course this is nothing new; people have been doing this since poor Eve added to the only instruction she and Adam received and said those fatal words, "We shouldn't even touch it." Today, we discuss and speculate on everything from Adam to Zachariah; we add things that aren't there and leave out important details that are there in those crucial verses effectively removing any original context of what is written for our instruction and understanding.

One teaching given by our Messiah was so controversial that many of those who were following Him "fell away," they left feeling offended by the truth He was telling them. Just like so many today these people heard His words but didn't believe what He was telling them. Arrogance and ignorance allow us so much comfort that when faced with the truth, that "Gospel that was once delivered to the saints," we think we have been betrayed. Well, we have been betrayed but not by God, we have been caught in the trap just like Eve, we have heard what we thought was Scripture but it was a twisted scripture. Something was added or removed to fit the purpose of a lie. Is it possible to crack through the hard shell of lies and get to the real truth? Yes it is, the question is; do you want to know the real truth?

Christians have a sense of destination; they all want to get into this place called Heaven. Unfortunately, too many want to ignore the journey or think they are able to find a short cut but that is for another lesson. Focus if you will on what happens between the time we leave this world and when we get to Heaven or the Kingdom of God. The Bible does not give a detailed description of what happens, when we read the complete context of Scripture there is a snapshot, a single picture of the time we spend between two places. What you are about to read is a close examination of what Scripture reveals in that picture, no, it is not controversial if you believe the Bible is the word of God but if you are comfortable in ignorance it can be offensive.

The writers of our "New Testament" were careful to let us know there is a difference between the Heaven where God lives, the heavens we see where the sun, moon and stars are and the Kingdom of God. We should be as careful when reading to know the difference; we should keep in mind what the Scripture reveals to us about who goes where and why.

To begin, death as described in the Bible is not a permanent state of being, death is temporary and most often described as being asleep. The following verses are just a few examples;

Daniel 12; 2 And many of them that sleep in the dust of the earth shall awake, some to everlasting life, and some to shame and everlasting contempt.

Job 3; 17 There the wicked cease from troubling; and there the weary be at rest.

Psalms 13; 3 Consider and hear me, O Lord my God: lighten mine eyes, lest I sleep the sleep of death;

There are at least a dozen places in the Old and New Testament which describe death as being asleep or at rest. Some of the others are; Psalms 90; 5, 2 Samuel 7; 12, Acts 7; 60, 1 Corinthians 15; 6, 18, 51.

All of these verses tell us that in this temporary place or state of being we are sleeping or resting after a life on this earth and before something greater. After all when we leave this mortal body wouldn't our soul enjoy and almost deserve a really good nap? So the question becomes; why do we look at this thing called death differently than what the Bible describes?

Language and translation problems occur when people either aren't quite sure how to best translate a word or idea into a different language or when there is a hidden agenda to be inserted into Scripture. There is a verse that is a great example and has been misused often, 2 Corinthians 5; 8 We are confident, I say, and willing rather to be absent from the body, and to be present with the Lord.

(KJV) Looking back into the Greek we see a different message; the Disciples' Literal Translation puts it this way; yet we are confident and prefer rather to get-away-from-home, out of the body, and to get-at-home with the Lord. This is close but still not as literal as it should be. The Greek word translated as "present" or "get-at-home" sounds like "pros" and a more literal definition is toward or moving to but you are not there yet. In the Greek Interlinear there is a different word which sounds like "paregenonto" used to describe as being in the presence of. A good verse to use as an example where both words are used is in Acts 21; 18 And the day following Paul went in with us unto James; and all the elders were present. In this verse we see people are moving toward a place while others are actually in their presence. Yes the moving toward "pros" is used and already in the presence "paregenonto" is used.

From this example there is a translation definition problem which has led to the misuse of this verse to mean that when we depart from this world we automatically pop up in Heaven. There is no Scriptural support for this theory! In fact quite the opposite is found in Scripture but first examine one of the Messiah's parables found in Luke 16; 19–31

19 There was a certain rich man, which was clothed in purple and fine linen, and fared sumptuously every day:

20 And there was a certain beggar named Lazarus, which was laid at his gate, full of sores,

21 And desiring to be fed with the crumbs which fell from the rich man's table: moreover the dogs came and licked his sores.

22 And it came to pass, that the beggar died, and was carried by the angels into Abraham's bosom: the rich man also died, and was buried;

23 And in hell he lift up his eyes, being in torments, and seeth Abraham afar off, and Lazarus in his bosom.

24And he cried and said, Father Abraham, have mercy on me, and send Lazarus, that he may dip the tip of his finger in water, and cool my tongue; for I am tormented in this flame.

25 But Abraham said, Son, remember that thou in thy lifetime receivedst thy good things, and likewise Lazarus evil things: but now he is comforted, and thou art tormented.

26 And beside all this, between us and you there is a great gulf fixed: so that they which would pass from hence to you cannot; neither can they pass to us, that would come from thence.

27 Then he said, I pray thee therefore, father, that thou wouldest send him to my father's house:

28 For I have five brethren; that he may testify unto them, lest they also come into this place of torment.

29 Abraham saith unto him, They have Moses and the prophets; let them hear them.

30 And he said, Nay, father Abraham: but if one went unto them from the dead, they will repent.

31 And he said unto him, If they hear not Moses and the prophets, neither will they be persuaded, though one rose from the dead.

The first problem is people do not understand that this is a parable, not something literal but an example. If this lesson was literal we could then assume the following;

1. When we die, angles carry us into the arms of Abraham to be coddled for eternity
2. People in hell are able to see those in Heaven and also witness the glory of God

3. People in hell are able to speak directly to those in Heaven begging relentlessly for mercy all the time
4. Those who have been given their reward in Heaven hear the cries of the tortured souls in hell

The purpose of this parable is not to describe Heaven but to teach us that if we do not listen to and believe Moses and the prophets we will not believe the Messiah either.

Another passage in Luke chapter 23 adds to the confusion. Yeshua tells the thief on the cross "truly I tell you today, you will be with me in paradise." The grammar in this verse changes with placement of the comma. Turning to the Greek texts we don't learn much either, however! KEEP READING! We learn that Yeshua was buried in the tomb and then rose on the third day; he did not go to paradise that same day as it appears he told the thief. Instead Yeshua was telling the thief "this day I tell you the truth, you will (*at some point in the future*) be with me in paradise." To claim anything else would be to say that the Savior was not telling the thief the truth. John 20; 17 Y'shuah warns Mary not to touch Him; why? Because He has NOT YET ASCENDED. There is no possible way if He had not been to Heaven that He would have been there with the thief. Also look at the word paradise, he didn't say heaven at all. What Yeshua did say was the thief would eventually be with him somewhere called paradise; when the earth is remade new in Revelation chapter 21. That is when John sees the new Heaven and new Earth; that is the paradise Yeshua was referring to

So far this examination of Scripture reveals that what we call death is both temporary and peaceful. We rest and wait and that wait is described best in Revelation 6; 9–11 9 And when he had opened the fifth seal, I saw under the altar the souls of them that were slain for the word of God, and for the testimony which they held:10 And they cried with a loud voice, saying, How long, O Lord, holy and true, dost thou not judge and avenge our blood on them that dwell on the earth?11 And white robes were given unto every one of them; and it was said unto them, that they should rest yet for a little season, until their fellow servants also and their brethren, that should be killed as they were, should be fulfilled.

These verses reveal that those souls who have been faithful are resting under the alter of grace and at some point God will speak to them and assure them that the time is getting closer for them to be raised into the glory of the almighty. What a vision! God will speak to His resting children!

So when do we get to Heaven? John chapter 6, the Messiah Himself answers the question in such a way that many of those who were with Him left. To put this into context we need to find out where He was and what had been happening just prior to this teaching.

After Yeshuah had fed the 5,000 he walks across the water (Matt.14 and Mark 6.) He and His disciples wind up in Capernaum where He teaches in a synagogue just before the first day of the seventh month, the feast of trumpets. Many who are there followed Him around the sea and by His words we learn they are there because he fed them bread and fish. His teaching continues and between verses 39–54 of chapter 6 Yeshuah emphasizes **4 times** that on the last day I will raise you up. Again many were offended by this teaching and went away, but those who stayed and were faithful were rewarded far above anything they could have imagined. Yeshuah later describes what the last day will be like in Matthew chapter 24.

Paul confirms this teaching in 1 Corinthians 15;21–23 21 For since by man came death, by man came also the resurrection of the dead.22 For as in Adam all die, even so in Christ shall all be made alive.23 But every man in his own order: Christ, the firstfruits, afterward they that are Christ's at his coming.

In verse 21 we see that everyone dies but there is a resurrection. In verse 23 we see everyone is raised in his own order, first is the Messiah, then the first fruits.

[So who are the first fruits? Remember at the crucifixion, the earth quaked and the rocks rent and the souls of many were seen in the streets (Matt 27, Mark 15, Luke 23.) These are the souls Yeshuah took to the throne room between the resurrection and His walk to Emmaus. The 24 Elders we see in the visions of the throne room after the Resurrection but not before, This is what Paul spoke of in Hebrews 10 about how Yeshua is our High Priest forever in the order of Melchezideck the righteous king (melech tzedek in Hebrew.)]

Now we see those who are the Messiahs' at His coming, those who are faithful, the ones who will be raised when the seventh trumpet sounds and the shout is heard. These are the souls who will take part in the marriage supper of the lamb and reign with the Messiah for 1,000 years on earth while Satan is bound.

Finally we will see the rest raised after the 1,000 year reign and the final defeat of Satan. These are the souls who will be judged either sheep or goats and that judgement takes place on earth not in Heaven. (Revelation chapter 20) Those people who either didn't get to hear the word of God or never had the chance to hear the truth but had a spirit that was trying to connect and hear His voice, they will be counted as sheep. Those who refused the word or had a spirit of evil will be judged as goats. Then after all of the unrighteous souls are removed and thrown into the lake of fire, those that remain will get to see what John saw in his vision. The earth made new and a new Jerusalem lowered to earth for the faithful to live in, with the glory of God, forever.

No, we don't get to live in the clouds, we don't get to lay around all day playing a harp and smoking a big fat cigar. Our eternity will be spent in the presence of the Messiah who will be God On Earth!

Many people want to take comfort in their ignorance of Scripture believing that when they die they will be immediately met by St. Peter at the pearly gates. This image of the pearly gates comes from the New Jerusalem found in Revelation and that hasn't been lowered to the New Earth yet. Is there comfort in a lie? Maybe, but there is far more comfort in the truth. While Heaven should be our destination, we should slow down and enjoy the journey. Using the Messiah as our example of how to live and love our neighbor, we see He was not in any hurry to go to the cross. Yeshuah was always ready to show mercy and do those acts of compassion personally. He never said "I'll give to the church so together we can make a difference." He was willing to get involved and to do what wasn't popular; when someone needed Him He was there.

The instructions we get from Heaven through Moses teach us how to live individually and as a community, when we follow those instructions our works reveal our fruit, our acts of compassion show our obedience and dedication to God, above any words. God doesn't want to hear we love, He wants to see that love; and that is the journey that leads down the narrow path in the footsteps of the Messiah. After all, His destination should be where we want to go, and the best way to get some place is by following the person who knows the way.

Now what about all of the stories we hear today from the people who have had near death experiences or from the loved one who have been left to face life without a loved one after they have passed from this life? Those visions are just exactly that, visions which the Holy Spirit has given them for comfort, reassurance and security. Those visions, not unlike those we see from some of the people we read about in the Bible are small glimpses, snapshots of a future event such as seeing a loved one with their arms around the Messiah or meeting a long passed relative. Those visions are very real and they have been given for a purpose. Throughout history we have been given tiny pictures of Heaven through the eyes of some very special people. Sometimes they are very detailed images and sometimes only vague almost blurred descriptions. Either way, until the Messiah returns to claim what is rightfully His, these visions are our only real picture of what we can expect this place called Heaven to look like.

ABOUT THE AUTHOR

JERRY MITCHELL CRAVES adventure, exploring the ocean and the mountins was only training for his greatest adventure; exploring the Bible. Digging through the language, culture and the history to discover the answers to the questions many people ask. With the tenacity of a hunting lion, he refuses to stop until every detail is justified, proven and can be explained without speculation. Not afraid and unoffended by the truth he continues to reveal answers to the difficult questions.